COLLEGE GOATs

THE GREATEST OF ALL TIME

GOATs OF COLLEGE FOOTBALL

BY CHRÖS McDOUGALL

SportsZone

An Imprint of Abdo Publishing

abdobooks.com

abdobooks.com

Published by Abdo Publishing, a division of ABDO, PO Box 398166, Minneapolis, Minnesota 55439.

Printed in the United States of America, North Mankato, Minnesota.
102025
012026

Cover Photo: Samuel Lewis/Corbis/Icon Sportswire/Getty Images
Interior Photos: Hulton Archive/Archive Photos/Getty Images, 5; Bettmann/Getty Images, 6, 9, 10, 13, 14, 18; Rich Clarkson/NCAA Photos/Getty Images, 17; UPI/Bettmann Archive/Getty Images, 20–21; George Gojkovich/Getty Images Sport/Getty Images, 22; Focus On Sport/Getty Images Sport/Getty Images, 25; Damien Strohmeyer/Allsport/Hulton Archive/Getty Images, 26; David Longstreath/AP Images, 28–29; Jonathan Daniel/Getty Images Sport/Getty Images, 30; Rick Stewart/Allsport/Getty Images Sport Classic/Getty Images, 33; Duane Burleson/AP Images, 34; Jamie Schwaberow/NCAA Photos/Getty Images, 37; John Korduner/Icon Sport Media/Icon Sportswire/Getty Images, 38; Christian Petersen/Getty Images Sport/Getty Images, 41; Don Juan Moore/Getty Images Sport/Getty Images, 42

Editor: Dalton Rains
Series Designer: Kate Liestman

Library of Congress Control Number: 2025939137

Publisher's Cataloging-in-Publication Data

Names: McDougall, Chrös, author.
Title: GOATs of college football / by Chrös McDougall
Description: Minneapolis, Minnesota: Abdo Publishing, 2026 | Series: College GOATs: the greatest of all time | Includes online resources and index.
Identifiers: ISBN 9781098298319 (lib. bdg.) | ISBN 9798384932116 (ebook)
Subjects: LCSH: College sports--Juvenile literature. | American football--Juvenile literature. | College football players--Juvenile literature. | College sports--Records--Juvenile literature.
Classification: DDC 796.33263--dc23

TABLE OF CONTENTS

JIM THORPE

Little about early college football would be familiar to fans today. The forward pass didn't become legal until 1906. Rules such as 100-yard fields, 15-minute quarters, and six points for touchdowns arrived a few years later. Yet even then, one great player could take over a game.

Jim Thorpe was born in 1888. A member of the Sac and Fox Nation, he grew up in an area that is now the state of Oklahoma. He later attended the Carlisle Indian Industrial School in Pennsylvania. During Thorpe's time there, Carlisle developed a reputation as a football power.

Thorpe attended Carlisle from 1907 to 1908, and again from 1911 to 1912. An all-around athlete, he thrived in just about every sport he tried. At the time, though, he was best known for his prowess on the football field. Playing under pioneering coach Pop Warner, Thorpe starred as a halfback and defensive back. He could run, punt, kick, pass, and catch. A famous sportswriter of the time marveled at Thorpe. He wrote, "There was nothing in football that he couldn't do well, and few things he couldn't do brilliantly."

After college, Thorpe became even more famous. He won the decathlon and pentathlon at the 1912 Olympics in Stockholm, Sweden. Both competitions involve multiple track-and-field events. Thorpe then went on to shine as a professional football and baseball player. Many still consider him the greatest athlete of all time.

In 1951, Carlisle's Jim Thorpe was voted into the first class of the College Football Hall of Fame.

Running back Red Grange averaged 5.3 yards per carry during his three seasons at Illinois.

RED GRANGE

College football exploded in popularity during the 1920s. Illinois running back Red Grange was a big reason for that. "The Galloping Ghost" escaped would-be tacklers with his elusive running style. If he reached the open field, there was no catching him. The blazing-fast Grange captivated fans with his long touchdown runs.

College athletes were allowed to play three seasons during Grange's era. He earned All-America honors in all three, from 1923 to 1925. However, Grange's fame really took off in 1924. In October of that year, Illinois dedicated its new Memorial Stadium. Classes were canceled the Friday before. Nearly 68,000 fans showed up for a Saturday game against Michigan. They were treated to one of the most legendary performances in college football history.

Grange received the opening kickoff at his own 5-yard line. Then he wove his way down the field for a score. A few minutes later, he took a handoff and ran for a 67-yard touchdown. Within 10 minutes, he'd added two more scores off 56- and 44-yard runs. By the end of the game, he had piled up more than 400 yards and scored five touchdowns as a rusher. He passed for another score. Grange even acted as the ball-holder for two extra-point kicks. It was a performance for the ages.

Grange played only 20 games at Illinois. Yet he racked up an amazing 3,362 yards and scored 31 touchdowns. The Illinois star had proven he was one of the greatest athletes of his era.

JOHN LUJACK

Under coach Knute Rockne, Notre Dame became an unlikely power. The small Catholic school in Indiana won three national titles in the 1920s. Along the way, the Fighting Irish developed a national following. Notre Dame remains one of college football's most popular and successful programs.

The Fighting Irish were at their most dominant in the 1940s. It was a difficult period in the United States. Many young men were called to fight in World War II (1939–1945). In 1943, quarterback Angelo Bertelli led the Irish to a 6–0 start. Then he left school to serve in the Marine Corps. Sophomore John Lujack stepped in to close out the 9–1 season. Notre Dame was voted national champion. After the season, Lujack left to join the Navy.

In 1946, Lujack was back at Notre Dame. The four-sport star picked up where he had left off. He could beat defenders on the run or with his passing arm. But he was also a great defender. He even punted sometimes. A huge crowd showed up to watch Notre Dame play Army in New York that year. It was called "The Game of the Century." Hobbled by injuries, Lujack threw three interceptions.

FAST FACT

One of Notre Dame's few down years came in 1956. The Fighting Irish finished 2–8. But do-it-all quarterback Paul Hornung still won the Heisman Trophy. He's still the only Heisman winner from a losing team.

But he also made a game-saving tackle. The teams ended up tying 0–0. Lujack's success made him a huge star. Before the 1947 season, he appeared on the cover of *Life* magazine. Lujack lived up to the hype. The senior went on to lead the Fighting Irish to a perfect 9–0 record. Over Lujack's three seasons, the team went 26–1–1. The Fighting Irish won the national title all three years. And in 1947, Lujack won the Heisman Trophy. That award is given each year to college football's best player.

Notre Dame quarterback John Lujack was an All-American in 1946 and 1947.

DICK BUTKUS

No ball carrier wanted to meet Dick Butkus on the gridiron. The 6-foot-3 Illinois linebacker was considered huge for his era. He was also ferocious. Anyone carrying the ball in his direction could expect a jarring hit.

Illinois linebacker Dick Butkus earned All-America honors in 1963 and 1964.

Butkus, a Chicago native, played as a center on offense. But he was most feared on the defensive side of the ball. From 1962 to 1964, he set a new standard for linebackers. Butkus chased down opponents as if they'd personally wronged him. The Fighting Illini went 2–7 in Butkus's first season. His aggressive play helped them improve to 8–1–1 in 1963. That year, in a tie against eighth-ranked Ohio State, Butkus recorded a school-record 23 tackles. Later, he snagged a key interception in a 17–7 win over Washington in the Rose Bowl.

By 1964, Butkus was established as an all-time great defensive player. He backed up his reputation with another standout season. Though Illinois finished just 6–3, Butkus was everywhere on the field. He ended his career with 374 tackles. College teams now play more games each season. Yet 60 years later, Butkus's career totals still ranked among the school's top 10.

FAST FACT

The Heisman Trophy was created in 1935. Even today, the finalists are almost always offensive players. But in 1964, voters ranked Butkus third. To this day, no linebacker has won the trophy. But since 1985, they've had their own, perhaps more fitting, honor: the Butkus Award.

ROGER STAUBACH

Roger Staubach didn't start out as a quarterback. It wasn't until high school that coaches had him switch to the position. The Cincinnati, Ohio, native didn't like it at first. But it was the right call. "Roger the Dodger" was just too good with the ball in his hands.

Nearby Ohio State wanted Staubach. Instead, he enrolled at the United States Naval Academy. The Midshipmen were one of the nation's strongest teams at the time. So were the Army Black Knights. The service academies' annual rivalry meeting is always a huge game. That was especially true in 1962, when President John F. Kennedy showed up to watch the game. Navy's first-year quarterback didn't disappoint.

Staubach could pick apart defenses with his strong passing arm. And the 6-foot-2-inch signal caller was just as good on the run. Opposing defenses didn't know what they had to stop until it was too late. With President Kennedy watching the game through binoculars, Staubach's Midshipmen charged to a 22–6 lead before winning 34–14.

That famous 1962 performance showed Staubach's potential. He put on more great performances in the 1963 season. Staubach piled up 1,474 passing yards and ran for another 418. Navy's 9–1 record in the regular season earned the team a No. 2 ranking. Top-ranked Texas finally slowed down the Midshipmen in the Cotton Bowl. Still, Staubach ended the season with just about every available award, including the Heisman Trophy. Injuries slowed down the senior in 1964. But he still left Navy with 28 school records.

Navy quarterback Roger Staubach posted 3,571 career passing yards.

JIM BROWN

Syracuse teammates nicknamed their star running back "First Down Brown." That's because when the ball was in Jim Brown's hands, it was a good bet that the officials would be moving the chains. From 1954 to 1956, Brown put up incredible numbers for the Orange.

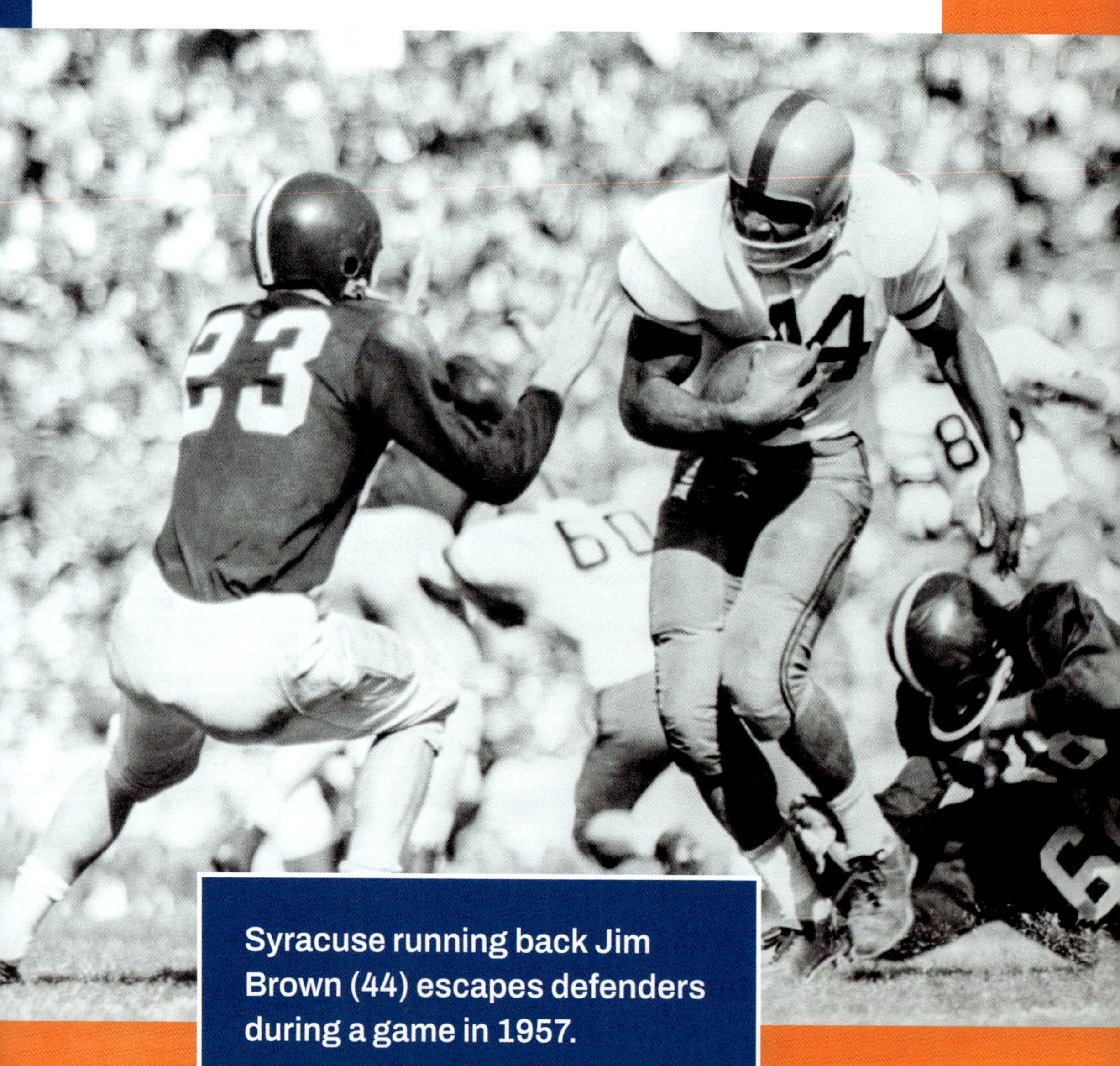

Syracuse running back Jim Brown (44) escapes defenders during a game in 1957.

Half a century later, a panel of 150 ESPN experts ranked him the best college football player ever. And yet, many at the time said football wasn't even Brown's best sport. The 6-foot-2, 212-pound Brown also starred in basketball, track and field, and lacrosse. Some consider him the best lacrosse player ever.

In football, Brown was a do-it-all star. He racked up yards as a kick returner. No one scored more touchdowns on kick returns in 1956. Brown also kicked extra points for the Orange. But he shone brightest as an explosive running back.

As a senior in 1956, Brown dominated the National Collegiate Athletic Association (NCAA). With an unstoppable combination of speed and strength, he averaged 6.2 yards a carry. Long, breakaway runs became the norm. Colgate University learned that the hard way in Brown's last regular-season game. He powered his way to six touchdowns and 197 yards. Including his seven extra points, Brown accounted for 43 total points. That set an NCAA record.

FAST FACT

Brown was only the second Black athlete to play football at Syracuse. He encouraged fellow running back Ernie Davis to follow him there. In 1961, Davis won the Heisman Trophy. He was the first Black player to earn the honor.

JOHNNY RODGERS

Coach Bob Devaney took over a losing Nebraska team in 1962. Over his 11 seasons, the Cornhuskers grew into a national power. Johnny Rodgers, a local star from nearby Omaha, Nebraska, helped the team reach its peak.

At 5-foot-9 and 173 pounds, Rodgers wasn't a huge player. But "The Jet" knew how to make defenders miss. As a wingback, Rodgers both ran with the ball and caught passes. His swift running also made him a terror on returns. *Sports Illustrated* compared tackling him to catching a bolt of lightning.

In 1970, Rodgers led Nebraska to 11 wins and the program's first national title. The Cornhuskers were even more dominant the next year. Their biggest test came in a Thanksgiving Day matchup against Oklahoma. Fans around the nation tuned in to watch the undefeated rivals spar. Early in the game, Rodgers fielded a punt at Nebraska's 28-yard line. His weaving 72-yard return opened the scoring. It became the iconic play of the Huskers' thrilling 35–31 win. In that season's Orange Bowl, he had another long return for a score. It helped Nebraska take down Alabama 38–6 to win its second national championship.

Nebraska fell short of a third national title in Rodgers's final year, but there was still no stopping the Jet. He piled up 290 total yards in one 1972 game. For the season, he recorded 1,978 all-purpose yards. In December, Rodgers became the first receiver to win the Heisman Trophy. But he wasn't done yet. His final game was back in the Orange Bowl. This time, Rodgers ran for three scores. He added another on a 50-yard catch. And he even threw for a 52-yard touchdown. The Huskers shut down Notre Dame so thoroughly that Rodgers got to sit out the fourth quarter of the 40–6 rout.

Wide receiver Johnny Rodgers returned seven punts and one kickoff for touchdowns during his three years at Nebraska.

Starting in 1973, Ohio State running back Archie Griffin led the Big Ten in rushing yards for three years straight.

ARCHIE GRIFFIN

The NCAA began allowing freshmen to play in 1972. That didn't change much for Woody Hayes. The Ohio State coach usually did not even let his sophomores play. Then Archie Griffin arrived. Not even the stubborn Hayes could ignore Griffin's talent.

Griffin had been born in Ohio State's hospital. He grew up in Columbus, then starred at the city's Eastmoor High School. Staying home for college, Griffin arrived in 1972 as a 5-foot-10, 185-pound tailback. Coach Hayes tried to ease Griffin into the team. The freshman did not get any carries in the season opener. But it soon became clear that Griffin would be impossible to hold back. In the Buckeyes' next game, he got a chance to take the field and proceeded to run for a school-record 239 yards.

With his low, forward-leaning running style, Griffin was tough to take down. It was as if his legs were moving one way and his shoulders the other. Griffin ran for 1,428 yards in 1973. That made him the first Buckeyes sophomore to break 1,000 yards in a season. In 1974, he exploded for another 1,620 yards and 12 touchdowns. Griffin followed that up with 1,357 more yards as a senior. Along the way, he became the first player to win back-to-back Heisman Trophies.

Hayes said that for all of Griffin's athleticism, the Ohio State star's attitude was his greatest asset. Griffin's impact showed in the standings. The Buckeyes reached the Rose Bowl in all four of his seasons.

EARL CAMPBELL

Some athletes get their strength from the weight room. Earl Campbell got his from the field. Growing up in Tyler, Texas, his family didn't have much money. Campbell and his 10 siblings worked long hours picking roses. The work made him strong and tough. And when "The Tyler Rose" arrived at Texas in 1974, he quickly became one of the best players in the nation.

At 5 feet, 11 inches and 220 pounds, Campbell packed extraordinary power into his frame. When his massive thighs began pumping, he was like a bowling ball rolling downhill. Campbell began as a fullback in Texas's wishbone offense. Coach Darrell Royal was happy to put the ball in the freshman's hands. In 1974, Campbell thumped his way to 928 yards and six touchdowns. He charged for 1,118 yards and 13 scores the next year.

Injuries limited Campbell as a junior in 1976. Before the next year, new Texas coach Fred Akers changed up the offense. The Longhorns still called on Campbell to bulldoze his way up the middle. But other plays allowed Campbell to take the ball out wide too. The result was a dominant senior season. Campbell led the nation with 1,744 yards and 19 touchdowns on the ground.

The Longhorns charged to a perfect 11–0 regular season. But the season ended on a sour note. Notre Dame upset the top-ranked Texas in the Cotton Bowl. Nonetheless, Campbell secured his place in NCAA history as the team's first Heisman Trophy winner.

Texas running back Earl Campbell scored 41 touchdowns over the course of 40 career games.

HUGH GREEN

At 6-foot-1 and 227 pounds, Hugh Green was small for a defensive end. That didn't seem to hold him back. Green announced his arrival at Pittsburgh with a dominant 1977 debut. He made 12 tackles and two sacks while blocking a punt against Notre Dame. And he didn't slow down after that.

Defensive end Hugh Green was a three-time All-American at Pittsburgh.

Green played the game at one speed—fast. And he was relentless. No matter what offenses tried to do, Green found a way to stop them. He slipped past would-be blockers with ease. Quarterbacks never knew when he was going to slam them to the ground.

The Panthers were at the peak of their powers in the late 1970s. In 1976, the year before Green arrived, they had gone undefeated for a national title. The team continued to pile up wins with their new defensive star. After Green helped Pitt to back-to-back 11–1 seasons in 1979 and 1980, some were calling him the greatest defensive player ever.

Award voters seemed to agree. Green took home the Maxwell, Walter Camp, and Sporting News player of the year honors. None had gone to a defensive end before. Green ended up finishing second in voting for the Heisman Trophy, but that was enough to make history. No defensive player had ever finished that high.

FAST FACT

Running back George Rogers of South Carolina won the 1980 Heisman Trophy. Hugh Green got revenge a few days later. The Panthers crushed the Gamecocks 37–9 in the Gator Bowl.

HERSCHEL WALKER

College football wasn't ready for Herschel Walker. The Georgia running back piled up 1,616 rushing yards in 1980. It was the most dominant season ever from a freshman back. And Walker was just getting started.

A multi-sport star from Wrightsville, Georgia, Walker decided to stay close to home for college. At 6 feet, 2 inches and 222 pounds, he was both big and strong. He was also a state-champion sprinter and had the speed to prove it. Put it all together and Walker had everything he needed to steamroll through defenders.

Walker took a good Georgia team to the next level. In 1980, with their freshman star in the backfield, the Bulldogs raced to a perfect 12–0 season. It ended with Georgia's first NCAA-recognized national title. At the time, Walker's third-place finish in the Heisman Trophy voting was the best-ever for a freshman.

Walker was even better as a sophomore. He rushed for 1,891 yards and 18 touchdowns. Both were among the top three in the country. That year, he finished as runner-up in Heisman voting. As a

FAST FACT

Herschel Walker was known as an elite athlete. He also ran track at Georgia. Later, he took up bobsledding. As a brakeman, his two-man sled finished seventh at the 1992 Winter Olympics.

junior in 1982, Walker's 1,752 yards and 16 touchdowns on the ground again put him among the nation's leaders. And he finally won the Heisman Trophy. Walker left Georgia following the season. By then, he'd set 41 school records and 11 NCAA records. The Bulldogs went 33–3 during his three seasons.

After the 1980 season, Georgia running back Herschel Walker ran for 150 yards and two TDs in the Sugar Bowl, despite having a separated shoulder.

BO JACKSON

No one had seen an athlete quite like Bo Jackson. He excelled at everything he tried, including three varsity sports at Auburn. Jackson batted over .400 for Auburn's baseball team. He sprinted his way to the NCAA Championships in the 100-meter dash too. But his ability on the football field excited Auburn fans most of all.

Auburn running back Bo Jackson (34) led his conference in touchdowns in 1983 and 1985.

Jackson had starred on both sides of the ball in high school. He even handled kicks. At Auburn, he quickly became the country's top running back. The 6-foot-2, 230-pound phenom punished defenders with his mix of strength and speed. As a sophomore in 1983, he ran for 1,213 yards and scored 14 offensive touchdowns. Both totals led the nation. Behind the star back, Auburn put up its first 11-win season. After being limited by injuries the next year, Jackson arrived for his senior season in 1985 with huge expectations.

Once again, Jackson shimmied and powered his way past would-be tacklers. This time, he led the nation with 1,786 yards and 17 touchdowns on the ground. He averaged more than six yards per carry. The only thing Jackson didn't do was play every game. He took himself out of two games that season with injuries, leading some people to think he was overly cautious. That wasn't an issue in the biggest game of the year, though. Facing rival Alabama, Jackson played through cracked ribs and rushed for 149 yards. Soon after, he won the Heisman Trophy. Then he was off to start pro careers in both football and baseball.

FAST FACT

Going into 1982, Auburn hadn't beaten Alabama in nine years. Trailing late, Auburn faced a fourth down at the goal line. Then the Tigers handed the ball to Jackson. The true freshman leaped over the line for a touchdown. The iconic "Bo over the Top" play lifted Auburn to a 23–22 win.

BARRY SANDERS

As a senior in high school, Barry Sanders had a chance to set a regular season record. Instead, he took himself out of the game. The team-focused running back didn't want to risk getting injured before the playoffs.

Sanders's selflessness might have contributed to him getting overlooked by college coaches. His 5-foot-8 frame didn't help, either. Even after Sanders ended up at Oklahoma State in 1986, he had to wait his turn. The Cowboys already had an All-America running back in Thurman Thomas.

Sanders was relentless on the practice field and in the weight room. By his junior season in 1988, there was no more holding him back. The Cowboys hosted Miami of Ohio in the season opener. Sanders took the opening kickoff 101 yards for a score. It was a taste of what was to come.

The 197-pound Sanders knew he couldn't overpower defenders with his size. Instead, he tricked them with lightning-quick stutter steps and dizzying spin moves. As soon as tacklers thought they had him, Sanders was suddenly running the other way. Defenses had to be ready for anything.

Texas A&M learned that the hard way in Week 2. Sanders broke free for a 57-yard touchdown on the first possession. He soon danced his way to another score on a 61-yard punt return. Huge gains like that became common for Sanders. He topped 300 rushing yards four times that season. Behind their superstar back, the Cowboys finished 10–2. Along the way, Sanders ran away with the Heisman Trophy too.

In 1988, Oklahoma State running back Barry Sanders set the NCAA record for most rushing yards in a season with 2,628.

ORLANDO PACE

Running into Orlando Pace was like running into a wall. The Ohio State offensive tackle stood 6 feet, 6 inches tall and weighed 330 pounds. Those who tried to beat the massive lineman often got flattened instead. That's how Pace earned the nickname "Pancake Man."

Ohio State offensive lineman Orlando Pace (75) was a unanimous All-American in 1995 and 1996.

An Ohio native, Pace had shown all the tools of a great lineman while in high school. Those abilities blossomed in college. The Big Ten named Pace its Freshman of the Year in 1994. One year later, he received the Lombardi Award as the nation's top lineman. No sophomore had won the award before. No player had won it twice, either. Pace made history when he did just that in 1996.

Pace possessed incredible strength. Great offensive line play is about more than raw power, though. Opponents raved about Pace's agility and blocking technique. These skills made him almost unmovable at the line of scrimmage. As the left tackle, Pace had the important job of guarding the quarterback's blind side. He didn't give up a single sack in 1995 or 1996. Pace could also get down the field on run plays. This ability to block linebackers and safeties made him the ultimate weapon.

With Pace anchoring the line, Ohio State went 11–2 in 1995. The Buckeyes finished second in the nation at 11–1 in 1996. After his junior season, Pace finished fourth in voting for the Heisman Trophy. It was the best placement for an offensive lineman since 1973. Pace left after that and became the top pick in the 1997 NFL Draft.

FAST FACT

Since 1965, most college football players have focused on either offense or defense. Pace became the third offensive lineman since then to finish top five in Heisman voting. Ohio State tackle John Hicks was runner-up in 1973. Nebraska center Dave Rimington finished fifth in 1982.

PEYTON MANNING

Before going pro, Archie Manning starred as a quarterback at Ole Miss. Many expected his son Peyton to follow the same path to NFL stardom. Instead, the younger Manning surprised many by choosing to play college football at Tennessee.

At 6-foot-5 and 222 pounds, Peyton Manning had the ideal size for a quarterback. He was also a confident signal caller and had a rocket for an arm. Manning quickly became an elite passer. In 1994, he led the Volunteers to a 7–1 record as a freshman starter. By his sophomore year, he was rewriting Tennessee's record books. He was also piling up wins. Manning led the Volunteers to an 11–1 record in 1995. One year later, they went 10–2. Many predicted he would be the first pick in the spring's NFL Draft. Instead, Manning surprised again by returning to Tennessee for his senior season.

Early in the 1996 season, the Volunteers lost to Florida. It was Manning's fourth loss to the Gators. But his dominant passing helped Tennessee rebound after that. Against Kentucky, Manning threw for 523 yards and five touchdowns. The team arrived at the Southeastern Conference (SEC) championship game with a record

FAST FACT

In 1995, Manning led Tennessee to a big win over Alabama. A TV interview forced him to miss the celebration. Manning made up for it in 1997. After beating Alabama again, he directed the Tennessee marching band for its famous song "Rocky Top."

of 10–1. Auburn raced out to a 20–7 lead. But Manning led a thrilling comeback. His 43-yard touchdown pass to Marcus Nash secured the 30–29 win. Tennessee's hopes for a national title ended in an Orange Bowl loss. Nonetheless, Manning had proven himself as one of the sport's all-time great passers.

During his career at Tennessee, quarterback Peyton Manning set 33 school records, seven conference records, and two NCAA records.

CHARLES WOODSON

Charles Woodson quickly established himself as a star at Michigan. The cornerback snagged five interceptions as a freshman in 1995. As a sophomore, he grabbed four more.

Defensive back Charles Woodson (2) recorded 16 career interceptions at Michigan.

Woodson also began returning kicks and punts that season. He even took regular snaps at wide receiver. The season ended with him earning All-America honors.

Fans had huge expectations for Woodson's junior year. Amazingly, he exceeded them. The Wolverines roared to a 6–0 start in 1997. Next up was a rivalry game at 15th-ranked Michigan State. At one point, the Spartans' quarterback tried to throw the ball out of play. Instead, Woodson made a leaping one-handed interception. It was one of two picks in the 23–7 victory.

Michigan kept on winning after that. Woodson's spectacular plays were a big reason why. The Wolverines remained undefeated when Ohio State came to town in late November. The fourth-ranked Buckeyes aimed to spoil their rival's perfect season. Instead, Woodson took over. A 37-yard catch set up Michigan's first touchdown. On a later possession, he grabbed an interception in the end zone. It was his seventh of the season. But his biggest play was a 78-yard punt return for a touchdown. Woodson's incredible game helped the Wolverines seal a 20–14 win.

A few weeks later, Woodson won the Heisman Trophy. That made him the first primarily defensive player to earn the award. And a few weeks after that, the Wolverines met Washington State in the Rose Bowl. Woodson broke up four passes. He also made a diving interception in the end zone. Once again, the Wolverines' versatile star came up big in the 21–16 win. It secured Michigan's first national title in 49 years.

REGGIE BUSH

Magic was in the air on November 19, 2005. It was the Saturday before Thanksgiving. The University of Southern California (USC) Trojans were riding a 32-game winning streak, and a crowd of 90,007 packed the historic Los Angeles Memorial Coliseum. Under the bright stadium lights, Reggie Bush put on a performance for the ages.

The star running back took his second handoff 65 yards, setting up a USC touchdown. From then on, something special seemed to happen every time he touched the ball. The 6-foot, 203-pound back appeared to glide past the helpless Fresno State defenders. Whenever someone came close, Bush seamlessly switched directions. The Trojans handed the ball to Bush 23 times. He took those carries 294 yards while scoring a pair of touchdowns. His electrifying night ended with win number 33 for the Trojans.

Bush had always been a star at USC. A dynamic runner and return man, he racked up tons of all-purpose yards as a freshman and sophomore. The Trojans finished both seasons as national champions.

FAST FACT

Bush became the fifth Trojan tailback to win the Heisman Trophy. Mike Garrett (1965), O. J. Simpson (1968), Charles White (1979), and Marcus Allen (1981) were the others. The program's historic success at the position earned USC the nickname "Tailback U."

With his shifty movement and great hands, Bush could break a huge play at any moment. He finished his career with an NCAA-record 7.3 yards per touch. He also won the Heisman Trophy as a junior in 2005. Bush's storybook career nearly finished with a third national title too. However, USC lost a thriller to Texas in the Rose Bowl. It marked only the second defeat in Bush's three years.

In 2005, USC running back Reggie Bush averaged 8.7 yards per rush.

Florida quarterback Tim Tebow recorded 533 total yards in the Sugar Bowl after the 2009 season.

TIM TEBOW

The 2006 Florida Gators already had a good starting quarterback in senior Chris Leak. Yet all season, the Gators also used true freshman Tim Tebow for more dual-threat options. That continued in the national championship game. Tebow threw a touchdown pass in Florida's blowout win over Ohio State.

There was no sharing the spotlight after that. Over his final three seasons, Tebow took the nation by storm. At 6-foot-3 and 255 pounds, he looked more like a linebacker than a quarterback. And he used his big body to bulldoze his way to huge gains. Defenders couldn't put all their focus on stopping him from running, though. Otherwise, Tebow could beat them with a pass. Tebow finished 2007 with 32 passing scores and another 23 on his feet. He was the first player to both throw and run for 20 touchdowns in a season. He also became the first sophomore to win the Heisman Trophy.

Tebow's abilities made him a star. His passion and leadership elevated his popularity even more. Whenever he took the field, fans knew Florida had a chance to win. From September 2008 through November 2009, the Gators did just that. Their 22-game winning streak set a school record. Along the way, Tebow led the team to a second national title following the 2008 season.

Alabama finally stopped the Gators in the 2009 SEC Championship Game. Tebow didn't sulk, though. Instead, he closed his career with a blowout win in the Sugar Bowl. His 482 passing yards on 31 of 35 attempts topped his previous best by more than 100 yards.

DeVONTA SMITH

DeVonta Smith knew he had the talent to be a great wide receiver. The problem was his size. At just 6 feet and 150 pounds, Smith was small for a receiver. He had a plan, though. Every time he saw his reflection, he dropped and did 10 push-ups. The exercise helped him pack on a few extra pounds of muscle. But his work ethic was more important. It helped the kid known as "Tay-Tay" become a star.

Alabama was loaded with talent when Smith arrived in 2017. Even so, his strong hands and route running were impossible to ignore. Alabama faced Georgia in that year's national championship game. The Crimson Tide were down by three in overtime. Facing second-and-26, quarterback Tua Tagovailoa launched a deep pass. Smith caught it in stride. His 41-yard touchdown clinched a 26–23 victory to take the title.

The soft-spoken Smith didn't always command attention. Injuries slowed him down as a sophomore. Then he quietly piled up 14 touchdowns as part of a dominant receiver group as a junior in 2019. But when opportunity arose the next year, Smith was ready.

Still one of the smallest players on the field, Smith leaned into his strengths. He prepared his body. He always knew just where to go. And when a pass came his way, he almost always caught it. The senior star ended the season with 117 catches for 1,856 yards and 23 touchdowns. All were NCAA records. He also added scores on the ground and from a punt return. He became the first wide receiver in 29 years to win the Heisman Trophy. Smith capped his college career with one more dominant performance in the national title game. Even though he missed most of the second half due to injury, he finished the game with 12 catches for 215 yards and three touchdowns. Alabama rolled to another championship.

Alabama wide receiver DeVonta Smith hauls in the game-winning touchdown in the national championship game after the 2017 season.

TRAVIS HUNTER

Travis Hunter was never afraid to do things his own way. In high school, he was the nation's top football recruit. All the biggest programs wanted him. Instead, Hunter chose Jackson State. The historically Black university plays in the Football Championship Subdivision. But the Tigers offered the super-athletic Hunter an uncommon opportunity. He could play as a wide receiver or as

Colorado defensive back Travis Hunter strikes the Heisman pose during a game in 2024.

a cornerback. The true freshman excelled in both. His coach, Deion Sanders, took a new job at Colorado in 2023. Hunter followed. The Buffaloes had been a losing team. Sanders leaned on Hunter to change that. The sophomore star had good size at 6-foot-1 and 185 pounds. He also had blazing speed and elite football instincts. With all that put together, Hunter immediately thrived in the tougher Big 12 Conference. Injuries forced him to miss 3.5 games that season. But his performance in the others was enough to make him an All-American.

Nothing could keep Hunter off the field in 2024. He played almost every snap on offense and defense. He even took the field 21 times on special teams. The result was an all-around performance the likes of which college football hadn't seen since the early 1960s. On offense, Hunter put together one of the best receiving seasons in Colorado history. That included a team-record 15 touchdown catches. Hunter was just as electric on defense. He made one of his four interceptions with a diving catch against Central Florida. To celebrate, he performed the Heisman Trophy pose. Not long after, the award was his. Hunter became only the second full-time defensive player to win. Along the way, he led the Buffaloes to their first winning record in eight seasons.

FAST FACT

Before coaching, Deion Sanders had been a versatile player. At Florida State, he excelled as a shutdown cornerback and returner. He finished eighth in the voting for the 1988 Heisman Trophy. He became a dominant NFL cornerback while also playing some snaps at wide receiver.

HONORABLE MENTIONS

BRONKO NAGURSKI

Nagurski excelled as a tackle on defense and a fullback on offense for Minnesota. In 1929, he became the first player to be named an All-American at two positions.

TOMMY NOBIS

Nobis, a two-way star with Texas, was especially dominant as a linebacker. The tackling machine was a key contributor on the 1963 team that won the Longhorns' first national title.

GALE SAYERS

One of the sport's first great running backs, "The Kansas Comet" averaged 6.5 yards per carry with the Jayhawks from 1962 to 1964.

WALTER PAYTON

A powerful yet well-rounded running back for Jackson State, Payton earned Black College Player of the Year honors in 1973 and 1974.

DERRICK THOMAS

Thomas, a feared and capable linebacker, recorded an NCAA-best 52 sacks while anchoring the Alabama defense from 1985 to 1988.

NDAMUKONG SUH

Suh was an ultra-strong and imposing defensive lineman for Nebraska. His dominant 2009 season included 85 tackles, 12 sacks, three blocked kicks, and an interception.

CAM NEWTON

After struggling to catch on at Florida, the dual-threat quarterback transferred to Auburn. In his lone season, he lifted the Tigers to the 2010 national championship.

JOE BURROW

Burrow's 2019 season at Louisiana State University was one of the best ever. The quarterback capped his record-setting year by throwing for 463 yards and five touchdowns in a national championship game victory.

GLOSSARY

agility
The ability to move quickly and easily.

dedicated
Held an event to officially open something.

draft
A system that allows teams to acquire new players coming into a league.

dynamic
Energetic and exciting; in sports, usually referring to an athlete with one or more outstanding skills.

elusive
Difficult to catch.

Football Championship Subdivision
A group of teams that make up the second-highest level of college football.

interception
A pass intended for an offensive player that is caught by a defensive player.

recruit
An athlete whom a college is interested in.

reputation
Something a person is known for.

rivalry
An intense and ongoing competition between two teams.

route
The path a receiver takes on a given play.

sack
A tackle of the quarterback behind the line of scrimmage before he can pass the ball.

MORE INFORMATION

BOOKS

Graves, Will. *GOATs of Football*. Abdo, 2022.

Stathes, Corbu. *Everything Football*. Abdo, 2024.

Zweig, Eric. *It's a Numbers Game! Football*. National Geographic Kids, 2022.

ONLINE RESOURCES

To learn more about the GOATs of college football, please visit **abdobooklinks.com** or scan this QR code. These links are routinely monitored and updated to provide the most current information available.

INDEX

ABOUT THE AUTHOR

Chrös McDougall is a sportswriter, author, and book editor. While in college, he covered the Missouri Tigers football team for *The Maneater* and the *St. Joseph News-Press*. McDougall now lives in Minneapolis with his wife, two kids, and a Heisman Trophy–worthy boxer named Eira.